FROM
SANCTITY TO SORCERY

AN AUTHOR'S GUIDE TO BUILDING BELIEF STRUCTURES AND MAGIC SYSTEMS

A TREVENA

ISBN: 9798664136388

Cover art by P&V Digital

From Sanctity to Sorcery is also available as an ebook Guidebook.

The content of the ebook is the same. It offers a more portable version of this workbook, and simply requires you to provide your own space for notes.

AUTHOR GUIDES SERIES

30 DAYS OF WORLDBUILDING
An Author's Step-by-Step Guide to Building Fictional Worlds

HOW TO DESTROY THE WORLD
An Author's Guide to Writing Dystopia and Post-Apocalypse

FROM SANCTITY TO SORCERY
An Author's Guide to Building Belief Structures and Magic Systems

HOW TO CREATE HISTORY
An Author's Guide to Creating History, Myths, and Monsters

COMPLETE WORLDBUILDING
An Author's Step-by-Step Guide to Building Fictional Worlds

angelinetrevena.co.uk/worldbuilding

CONTENTS

INTRODUCTION

I am one of those authors who have been writing, pretty much, since they were old enough to hold a pen. I have a folder of old stories, typed up on an old typewriter, that I don't even remember having written.

I was rarely seen without a book in my hand, and spent every spare hour I had, buried deep in fantastical worlds. I was lucky in that my parents encouraged it. They never told me that I was wasting my time, or to keep my head out of the clouds. They even let me read at the dinner table, eating one-handed.

I was also lucky to have access to a local library, and quickly worked my way through the fantasy catalogue in their children's section. I swept my way through all of the Choose Your Own Adventure books; not only following the adventures of kids— passing into a fantasy world to fight dragons, mounted on their bicycle steeds—but I got to control the stories. I could re-read them over and over, choosing different paths each time, creating a multitude of adventures for myself.

My love of speculative fiction had started young. It was my dad's job to read the bedtime stories each night, all of us huddled together to listen. He often picked books from his own collection which, almost exclusively, consisted of classic sci-fi novels. And so, as a child, my bedtime stories were written by the likes of H.G. Wells and John Wyndham. Looking back, I suspect that *The War of the Worlds* and *The Day of the Triffids* were probably inappropriate choices for children about to go to sleep, but it must have caught my imagination. I will forever thank my dad for introducing me to such tales.

At the age of 16 I finally picked up the Chronicles of Narnia books, reading all seven of them in just five days. It was then that my Narnia obsession began, and it has never waned.

Before starting at university, I worked in an antique auction house. Every wardrobe that came through the saleroom, I would check in the back of it for Narnia. It reached the point that the staff would come and inform me each time they took receipt of one!

When they announced the latest film adaptations, I scoured the internet daily for news. I saw each of them on their day of release, going to the cinema alone for an uninterrupted experience. A pure absorption of them. I can still name the four actors who portrayed the Pevensie children, their names branded into my memory. Yes, the woman who can't even remember her own phone number!

One of my most treasured possessions is an old wardrobe. I bought it from a second-hand furniture shop for just £20. It has moved house with us several times, and has practically fallen apart, with my husband tasked with fixing it back together. Carved into its door is a beautiful rendering of a ship, in full sail, riding the sea. And the serpentine hinges on it are like sea monsters. It is beautiful, and largely useless. It isn't deep enough to hold a standard coat hanger on its rail, and the mirror on the back of the door is so mottled and degraded it hardly reflects anything at all. In fact, it has rarely ever been used as an actual wardrobe, and currently holds my increasingly out of control to-be-read pile.

But, because it looks like it may have once stood in the captain's quarters on board the Dawntreader, I will never part with it.

And, over the years, I have collected other bits and pieces that remind me of Narnia. Including film props, and a good collection of behind-the-scenes and the-making-of books. My obsession is complete, and incurable. All that is left is to find a way to Narnia myself. I'm still looking, and I won't give up.

As for my interest in religion, well, I wasn't brought up in a religious family; rather, by parents who routinely wrote 'Church of England' on forms simply because it was the done thing. But my best friend was a Christian, and attended the local Methodist church every Sunday. When I was around 8 years old, I asked my parents if I could go with her. And so, I became a regular churchgoer, along with my sister.

I can't claim to have ever been particularly 'devout', and I was far more interested in the social side of the church rather than the spiritual side of it. I made lots of solid friends through the church, and I met boys. We went to local events, national events, and it was a really fun part of my childhood.

But, still, I couldn't make myself interested in the religious side of things.

I was a typical teenage misfit; completely obsessed with the X-Files, huge crush on David Duchovny, and just beginning to discover punk music. I read extensively about conspiracy theories, paranormal events, myths and legends. I believed in ghosts, and fairies, and dragons. None of that quite suited the church. I was a jigsaw piece that didn't quite fit. In fact, at times, I was completely at odds with it.

That sense of displacement was exacerbated when I studied for my Sociology A-Level, and I was introduced to Marxism. The teachings of Karl Marx seemed to explain and corroborate the hypocrisy and double-standards I'd witnessed within the church community. Teaching forgiveness and acceptance with one breath, and casting judgements and prejudice in the next. Paradoxically, it pushed me further away from organised religion, while increasing my fascination with it from a sociological point of view.

I became more interested in the occult, watched The Craft back to back, and started to look enthusiastically at Paganism and Wicca. I can't imagine that shift surprised anyone. By my late teenage years and early twenties, I had drifted away from the church altogether, instead joining spiritualism and psychic development groups.

I've not been able to settle into a 'religion', preferring to take bits and pieces from here and there as the mood takes me. I've had people describe me as 'non-religious', which is true, but they often understand that to mean that I 'don't believe in anything', which is completely untrue. I definitely believe in something. In fact, lots of things. Probably too much. It's all a bit of a confusing mess, to be frank.

All I know is that I cannot accept that this one life is all we have. I can't quite believe that all existence came about by a random reaction between two random atoms, or whatever. I believe in some higher power, whether they are listening, intervening, puppeteering, or have forgotten about us altogether, I don't know. I believe in the things I've seen, and the things I've experienced, yet I remain sceptical of it all.

I'm a questioner. Or, perhaps more aptly, a questioneer. Yes, I like that. That sums things up nicely.

In the meantime, I will continue to be as drawn to the awe-inspiring majesty of cathedrals as I am to the thrumming power of stone circles.

USING THIS WORKBOOK

If you're looking to create belief structures and magic systems for your fantasy world, this is the book for you. If you'd like to deepen and expand your world's beliefs and magic, this is the book for you. If you're not sure where to start with creating these aspects to be believable and realistic, this is definitely the book for you.

This workbook is broken into several easy, manageable prompts for you to complete. If you work your way through, simply completing one prompt per day, then in just over a month, you will have a strong, solid basis to your world's belief structures and magic systems. From there, you can grow it more.

Each prompt has two spaces for you to write notes in. One space for magical notes, and one space for notes on religions and beliefs. If you prefer to merge everything together, please feel free. The important thing is that you use this workbook, and its space, in a way that is useful to you.

You'll notice that I've split the contents into three sections: **Fitting into Society**, **Nuts and Bolts**, and **The People**. It was an agonisingly difficult decision as to which order to place these sections in. Let me explain the conundrum. When it comes to worldbuilding, it's so important to keep reminding yourself that everything is intertwined. Nothing exists in isolation. Change an aspect of one thing, and it changes how it fits into your wider world, therefore changing the wider world. It is, in every way, a butterfly effect.

And so, in order to know how to create your belief structures and magic systems, you need to know how they fit into your world. You need to know how they change the people following them, and how those people fit into society. Society effects these institutions, just as the institutions effect society. So, what do you need to focus on first? The human aspect? The nuts and bolts of the institutions? Their place in your world? To be honest, that isn't something I can answer for you. Do your stories start with a character idea, a setting, or a situation? We're all different, and, oftentimes, this varies story by story. So, you see, it's impossible for me to speculate.

The reason I chose to place the Fitting into Society prompts first, is to show you the importance of integrating your belief and magic systems into your society. They can't be something you bolt on afterwards as an interesting piece of cultural flair. They need to feel like they exist and belong in your world. That your world wouldn't be the same without them. And so, I chose to put those sections in first.

But, you might not want to work that way, and that's fine. If you'd rather work through the Nuts and Bolts prompts first, or The People prompts, please do. If you want to jump around throughout all three sections, feel free. But, please know that how your systems fit into your world are of utmost importance. Whatever order you choose to work through this book, don't skip that part.

This list of prompts is not, by any means, exhaustive. Depending on your genre, your story, your characters, and the world you need to create for them, you may need aspects that are not covered by this workbook. Likewise, some of these prompts may not be relevant to you.

Think of it like a garden. This book gives you the foundation to build upon. It helps you to plant the seeds, and offers you seeds you may not have considered planting yourself. But, you'll need to cultivate it, and water it. And, you may have plants of your own that you want to include. A special tree, your favourite flower. You may like to have a pond, or a bench, or a marquee.

The other thing this workbook offers is a safe, singular place to keep all of your worldbuilding notes. It's surprisingly easy to get lost in your own world, and surprisingly easy to forget the details of it. This will become your worldbuilding bible. Your one-stop-shop for everything you need to know about your world's beliefs. When you come to writing your story, keep this book next to you, so that everything you need to know is in easy reach.

I have purposefully left the work pages of this book as blank as possible, because we all like to work in different ways. Draw pictures, create tables and graphs, or fill it with neatly written notes. Use it in the way that works best for you.

Above all, enjoy your worldbuilding. Enjoy exploring it, and watching it come to life around you.

As a simple human, this may be the closest you'll come to performing real magic. To visualise an entire world from nothing. To pluck things from the air and make them real. To take breath on the wind and form it into something tangible. That is the most real, purest magic I know of.

Of course, I'm being presumptuous here. You may have magical abilities beyond my comprehension. In fact, you may even be a little more than human...

WORLDBUILDING BASICS

While fantasy and science-fiction authors may be doing the heavy lifting when creating their fictional worlds, worldbuilding exists in, pretty much, every genre. To a certain extent.

Whether it's the creation of an imaginary cafe in a real town, or imagining an alternative outcome to an event from history, any book, of any kind, can involve worldbuilding. At the fantasy, sci-fi, and horror end of the scale, the worldbuilding-heavyweights, it may mean the creation of a magic system, or monsters, to slot alongside the real world. Or it may mean building an entirely new world with new species and cultures, right up to an entire universe of planets.

It can become quite the epic task!

Now, I don't know about you, but I tend to get easily overwhelmed by epic tasks. That's why I'm still working up to de-cluttering my house. I just look at the job as a whole, can't untangle where to actually start, and I end up doing nothing at all.

As much as I understand the usefulness and the importance of breaking things down into workable chunks, into simple steps, the ability and method for doing this very often escapes me. Unlike many other people, I can see the wood very clearly. It's the trees I have trouble with.

Worldbuilding doesn't need to be difficult, or complicated. It doesn't need to take forever, or be an excuse for never actually writing the book. It doesn't need to be overwhelming or intimidating. At the other end of the scale, it shouldn't be something that you haphazardly bolt on in a last-minute panic.

As you'll discover through this book, worldbuilding should be tightly integrated with your plot and your characters. Your characters, and their goals, their struggles, their journey, that is the reason your readers show up. That's the reason they keep reading. You can have the most amazing world, but if you don't populate it with compelling, sympathetic, and relatable characters, readers will simply stop turning the pages. Likewise, if you write amazing characters, and put them into a flat, paper world, your readers won't want to walk along with them, or explore with them.

Just as you want your readers to believe in your characters, you want them to believe in your world, too.

Let them smell the salt on the breeze, hear the buzzing of the insects. Let them feel the cavernous size of your temples, and the tingle of magic in their fingertips. Let them walk every single step with your characters. Invite them in. And invite them to stay. Whether they want to set up home there, or fight to change it.

Your worldbuilding is equally as important as your story and characters. Give your characters somewhere real to live, and give your readers somewhere real to visit. You simply can't separate these things out if you want to write the best book that you can.

So, what are you waiting for? Let's get started with the basics of worldbuilding.

DIFFERENT TYPES OF WORLDBUILDING

There are a few different ways to approach worldbuilding, and which you choose, will depend on your goals, your story, and your genre.

Building a whole new fictional world:
This is mostly used for writing fantasy and science fiction, and involves creating an entirely fictional world from scratch. Somewhere that does not, and never has, existed. It may have similarities to our world, and it may have huge differences. Think along the lines of second-world fantasies penned by the likes of J.R.R. Tolkien or C.S. Lewis.

A real place with an alternative past or future:
This may be taking a real existing place, London, for example, and giving it an alternative or altered history. Imagine if the Great Fire of London had actually been started by dragons. How would that change the world today? Or it may be taking the real-world place, and throwing it into your imagined future. This is very common in dystopia, imagining an unpleasant future for our world.

A real place with a parallel fictional world:
The other way is to set your story in a real place, and have a fictional world created alongside it, usually invisible or hidden from the general public. Such as in Neil Gaiman's Neverwhere, or Harry Potter, or Hellboy. The fictional side of the world may be tightly integrated with the real world, or it may be quite separate. This would depend, again, on your story.

Whichever kind of world you're building, your objective is still the same: to create a believable world that your readers can really imagine walking around in.

MAP MAKING

One of my favourite parts of worldbuilding is making the map. You don't need to be an amazing artist; a child-like scrawl on the back of an envelope is good enough, as long as it makes sense to you so that you don't end up getting lost in your own world. Which, believe me, is surprisingly easy.

Imagine your characters are travelling from A to B. If, in one chapter, B lies west of A, and then, suddenly, it's south, your readers will notice. Or if B is a coastal town one minute, and a village in the mountains the next, your readers will notice, and it will drag them out of your story. Plus, they will love to call you up on it. They'll email you. They'll message you on social media. And they'll write it in their reviews.

As an author, your job is to keep them in the story. To keep them believing that it's real. To blur out their real world, their real life, and construct a new one for them, for as long as they're reading your book. Glaring inaccuracies will pluck them out of your world. Inaccuracies break the illusion, and remind them that they are simply reading a story. That they're not a hero fighting against a terrible foe. It pulls them back to their own cold, harsh, boring reality. And no one wants that!

And so, at the writing stage, your world map is for you. If you're not confident in your artistic abilities, there are plenty of artists who can create a stunning map to go into the front of your book. At this stage, the map is only for your eyes. Build it out of Lego, build it on Minecraft, mould it from clay, or cake, or whatever. As long as it's useful to you (and you're not tempted to eat it!)

And don't be tempted to simply draw a map and then randomly scatter towns across it. That doesn't happen, it's not believable. Towns are founded in specific places for specific reasons. The main reason being, of course, survival.

So, imagine you're choosing a place to establish a town. What do you need? What considerations do you need to make?

Fresh water source:
The most important and first consideration. Have you ever noticed how many major cities have a river flowing through them?

Varied food source:
Man cannot live by bread alone. Or cake, sadly. Their food source needs to be varied enough to keep them healthy.

Natural resources:
They need enough resources to be able to build their homes, and the things they need. They can also use these resources for trade.

Appropriate land for crops/animals:
The landscape they choose to settle in will hugely impact the kind of food and animals they farm.

Access and security:
Can they get in and out of their settlement easily while still keeping it protected from intruders?

Trade route:
Can traders visit their settlement? Is it on a major trade route, or will they have to rely on people making a special trip?

Predators:
What lives in the woods? Or the mountains? How do they protect themselves against it?

People, by and large, will choose the easiest option for their home, unless the benefits outweigh the dangers or struggles. For example, you might consider it foolish to establish a town in the middle of a dragon breeding ground. But what if just one dragon scale (which could be naturally shed) would sell for a price that could feed a family for three months. Then, it may well be worth it.

NAMING PLACES

There are several different ways to name the places on your map. Remember that it's not just towns and cities you need to name. Depending on how big your map is, you might be naming mountain ranges, rivers, forests, counties, countries, oceans, continents, or even planets.

Just like places on your map aren't randomly placed, neither are they randomly named. They might be named after their founder, or the landscape, or the natural resources, the wildlife, the river or mountain they're close to. They might be named after a local legend; your place names can actually conjure up stories of their own.

Of course, you can backward engineer these things. You can find the name for a place, and then create the reason it was named that. Perhaps no one remembers. Perhaps it doesn't matter to you, or your characters, or your story. As I'll discuss in the next section, you don't need a full and complete history for everything.

There are so many online naming generators. Simply do a search, and you'll find countless. I have two that I favour:

- squid.org/rpg-random-generator
- seventhsanctum.com

HISTORY

Your current world is a product of everything that ever happened there, even if no one in your world still remembers. It's your job, as the writer, to know. To remember what they can't.

I'm not saying that you need to plot out 5 million years' worth of history. Unless you're into that. Some people are. But you definitely need to know enough to understand why things are the way they are. To know enough to effectively create the world, its culture, and values.

As people, we act according to our culture. And each culture is different. And there are variations in that culture. The things we value. The things we see as rude, or polite, or unnecessary. The things we want, the things we avoid. Religion. Festivals. The way we treat our elderly. The way we treat children. The kind of food we eat, and the way in which we eat it. The kind of jobs we do. The differences between rich and poor. The differences between high culture and low culture.

And these things change over time. Invading cultures. Migrating cultures. Important events. A war, or a natural disaster can hugely change a place's culture. Changing what's important to them. Changing the way they live their lives.

And you need to remember that every time something changes, it affects everything else.

There are different levels at which an event can occur.

International events:
Something that affects the entire world. Like climate change, population explosion, the sun dying, zombie apocalypse, etc.

National events:
Something that affects the country or large area. Like an economic crash, natural disasters, death of a monarch, etc.

Local events:
Something that affects a town or community. Harvest failure, flood, local elections, introduction of a new predator, a new trade deal, etc.

Individual events:
Something that affects one person or family. Bereavement, loss of employment, loss of home, births, marriages, a lottery win, etc.

It's obvious how an international event affects everything else. I'm sure a worldwide zombie outbreak would affect you and your family. But what about the other way round?

So, imagine a family preparing for a wedding. They order a whole load of wine from the next village. That gives the farmer enough money to finally live out his dream of buying a boat and exploring the seas. When the winter rains come, the lack of the vineyard on the hillside causes a landslip which demolishes the mining town below, which leads to a shortage of minerals, which leads to a shortage of coins, which results in an economic crash.

This is, of course, a somewhat extreme example, but it's an important thing to bear in mind. Think about the butterfly effect, and the ripples you might be sending out.

Imagine your world as a pool. Every event, ever construct, every thing you change or create, is like dropping a pebble into the water. Sometimes, the ripples last a few minutes. Sometimes, a few years. Spreading wider. Affecting more people. Sometimes, those ripples last for centuries.

HOW YOUR WORLD AFFECTS CHARACTER AND STORY

You can also use your worldbuilding to create conflict. Remember that conflict is created when your protagonist's goal is interrupted, or opposed, and you can use your world to do that.

Perhaps the most obvious example is if the protagonist's goal requires them to break the law. But you can use other things too: limitations of magic, social norms and expectations, gender roles. The landscape itself can become a physical barrier, or the weather, or a lack of resources.

And you can use all of this in your worldbuilding to raise the stakes. To increase the tension.

Because your world doesn't exist separately from the people who live in it, and you should create it with those people in mind. They will have opinions about everything. Beliefs, hopes, grievances. Things they love, things they hate. Things they want to change. Things they fight to change.

And these things will differ based on all of their nuances: gender, age, class, religion, etc. So their opinions will be different to the person stood next to them. They may even directly oppose one another. Conflict.

You have to remember that everything comes back to character. You have to remember that you aren't writing a story about a world that happens to have people living in it. You are writing a story about people who happen to live in a particular world.

Worldbuilding. Story. Character. None of these is independent from the others.

RELIGION AND MAGIC ALONGSIDE ONE ANOTHER

You may wish to create a belief system for your world, without adding any magic into it at all. Or you may want a magic system without any kind of religion or belief structure. Alternatively, you might want to create both for your world, even if one is resigned to the sidelines.

Remember that belief structures aren't necessarily a religion, but, for the purpose of this book, we're talking about beliefs that have a religious-like following. Something that affects how people live their life. That belief, however, may be atheism, or agnosticism. It may be a belief in spiritualism, clairvoyancy, they may be humanist or scientific beliefs. They may be lifestyle beliefs about sexuality, diet, abortion. Anything. Anything from which you can build a devout following or create an organised institution from.

And so, when this book talks about religion, know that it doesn't have to, literally, mean an organised, deity-based religion. Merely, an institution that teaches a specific set of beliefs to devout followers.

Religion and magic are not mutually exclusive. You can, absolutely, have both, and they can be as tightly wrapped around one another as you want.

Basically, you have three main choices, with, of course, an entire gradient of different shades in between each one.

Opposing forces: Magic and religion are at odds with one another. Religion doesn't accept the use of magic, and magic turns its back on religion. This option gives opportunities for playing with conflict (the basis of any story), from snide remarks, through demonstrations, prejudice, petitioning for a ban, right up to full-out war.

It also gives great opportunity for internal conflict within your characters: someone brought up in a deeply religious family who discovers a talent for magic, or someone brought up in a magical community who is spoken to by God.

At the other end of the scale, we have...

Fully integrated: Religion and magic don't exist without one another. Magic is part of the religious rituals, and magical rites are deeply religious. Believers practice magic as part of their religion, and magical practitioners are deeply religious.

But, this doesn't necessarily make for a peaceful situation. For one thing, it's likely that you would have different religions in your world, or different versions of the same religion. Likewise, you might have more than one magic system, or more than one way of practising magic.

And there is still lots of room for internal conflict. Characters who want to practice magic, but can't seem to find faith in the religious side of things. Or deeply religious characters who find magic distasteful, or difficult, or impossible to do altogether.

And, for all of those greys in between, you have magic and religion...

Co-existing: This is everything that comes in between, from a general tolerance of one another, to an ignoring of each other, up to them barely even registering the existence of the other.

It might be that either magic or religion is conducted in hiding, or in secret, or is thought of as nothing more than legend or rumours.

It might be that, centuries ago, after years and years of bitter war, religion and magic called a truce. That truce may be sealed in stone, or it may be precarious and ready to break at any moment. Things might change within religion or magic themselves to break the balance, or outside forces; such as government policy, or a change in the law, or the introduction of a new religion or magic system, may change things completely.

Perhaps religion and magic are forced to put their differences aside to become allies in a fight against a greater power.

There can also be smaller skirmishes between individual characters. People being excluded, ostracised, disapproved of. Bullying, rival gangs, or lovers unable to be together because they exist on opposing sides of the religion/magic divide.

Whichever option you choose, there is plenty of space for conflict, try/fail cycles, antagonists, barriers, and character arcs.

Write some notes below for both religion and magic, thinking about how they interact with one another in your world. You may use one page for notes on religion, and the other page for notes on magic, or you may merge your notes together. It is entirely up to you.

HOW SOCIETY INFLUENCES RELIGION AND MAGIC

One thing I keep repeating about worldbuilding is this: everything that exists in your world is connected to everything else. And the same goes for religion and for magic. There are many ways in which society could influence the religion and magic in your world.

It is likely, although not necessarily the case, that both religious and magical institutions and communities are still bound by the law of the land. While they may have their own, internal rules, regulations, and codes, the law of the land will overrule those of their institution or community.

It may be that, leaders of certain religions, or powerful practitioners of magic are largely untouchable by the law. They may have influence or abilities that place them outside of its reach. Alternatively, the law might delight in punishing such people for their indiscretions, hitting them with the harshest punishments in order to make an example of them.

Beyond laws, religion and magic may be controlled, moulded, or pressed upon by other societal institutions, such as education, employment, or economics. For example, religious leaders may encourage, or even require, charitable donations from its followers in a country that is still rebuilding after war or famine. In the same way, magical practitioners may be required to assist with a war effort, or to increase food production.

The basic principles of the religious teachings, or the magical code, may have been translated, rewritten, edited, or reinterpreted in a way to benefit one section of society. They may be used to oppress a particular demographic of people: to keep the poor from rising up the ranks, to keep women in the home, or to retain a particular race as slaves. Perhaps only affluent schools are permitted to teach magic, creating a system where only the wealthy can wield its power. If society wants something, it may have the sway and influence to bend the institutions' practices to its will.

Think, also, about how things may have changed over time. As society has changed, how have religion and magic followed? Have they moved along with it, or fought against it? Perhaps it is the wider society that is only just beginning to catch up.

Perhaps your society has improved its technology, reducing a requirement for magic. Maybe society has become more tolerant and liberal, impressing changes upon the religious hierarchy. If medical knowledge has greatly improved conventional medicine, the magic community may have been pushed aside. Magical remedies might fall out of fashion, become ridiculed, or be outlawed altogether.

Consider what drives people in your society. Is it a pursuit for wealth? Power? Knowledge? Peace? With everyone striving for the same things, jostling for the top position, how have religion and magic been bent and adapted to help certain people rise? Or are they holding strong to their opposing principles?

Use the spaces below to brainstorm the ways in which your society may have influenced religion and magic. Have they been co-conspirators in a rise to power, or have they been pushed aside, repositioned as unfashionable and undesirable as their usefulness in society has run out?

HOW RELIGION AND MAGIC INFLUENCE SOCIETY

In the same way that society has influenced religion and magic, so too, religion and magic may have helped to shape the wider society. As I've said; nothing in your world exists in isolation. Different aspects push and pull against each other, they rub together, they chafe.

Either religion, or magic, or both (whether simultaneously, or at different points throughout history) are likely to have had a significant impact on your society. If you think about the world you live in, right now, you can likely mention many points in history where society has been changed, sometimes irreversibly so, by religion. It has started wars, it has persecuted people, carried out genocide. Of course, we need to be careful here. Because, it isn't fair to say that religion itself has caused such things. It has been, perhaps, a catalyst, also a scapegoat, an excuse. A belief system, itself, cannot wield a sword, but a person can do so in its name, whether welcomely or not.

The laws of many countries are based on, or incorporate, the rules of their main religion. Their national anthems, their ideology, culture, and values often stem from religious ideology. Religion has also acted as a muse for architects, painters, and musicians. It is present in schools, in government. And it still acts as a beacon of hope, as a sanctuary, as a place to turn in times of upheaval and profound trauma. People mark the most important moments in their lives in religious buildings; births, coming-of-age rituals, marriages, deaths. Even people who aren't 'practising' in a particular religion opt to mark these moments there. Feeling that it, perhaps, gives them more weight and credence. Or, perhaps, out of a sense of duty or expectancy.

You can also apply this same influence on society to your magic system. Wars may well be fought over magic. It may be used to oppress and ostracise certain demographics of people. It may be the cornerstone of your whole society. The government may be made up of magic practitioners, the royal family may use magic. It might be a measure of someone's worth, of someone's role in the world.

Again, also consider how this influence may have changed over time. Has magic pushed its way into schools, or removed itself from the curriculum, reducing those able to use it? Has it seeped into government, or pushed its gender role expectations onto the wider population?

Has society happily accepted the influence of religion and magic? Perhaps the changes were made slowly, and subtly, with little resistance because people simply didn't notice it happening. Maybe there was civil war, with parts of society fighting back. Perhaps they fought fiercely, with losses on both sides, or it may have been an unfair fight, turning into a massacre.

Have things settled down, or is there still dissension, rebel groups, skirmishes, civil war? Perhaps people have discovered a way to fight back. Or maybe they welcome the new order, laws, and governance. Perhaps religion and magic have made things better.

Brought affluence to a struggling nation. Brought peace, or lowered soaring crime rates. Or maybe that's only happened in some areas, while others are pushed further and further into desperation.

Use the following space to write notes on the ways in which religion and magic have influenced the wider society, and how society has reacted to that influence.

WEAPONISING RELIGION AND MAGIC

Religion and magic, their principles, their institutions, their practices and power, can all be weaponised, either against people of another nation, or against their own people.

They can be weaponised by the institutions themselves, or by the government or rulers, or they can be weaponised by a group of people, either inside or outside of the religious or magic institution itself.

Let's look at some ideas of how this can play out.

A magical or religious institution can weaponise itself. It can impose itself, through physical force or through political ideology, it can impose its rules and regulations, its beliefs and prejudices. It can control an entire society, country, world. It can oppress, and divide, and create a dystopia of inequality and despair. It can kill and destroy and crush any opposition. They can force themselves into a position of power, and rule over whichever corner of the world they choose to.

The practices and ideologies may be weaponised by the country's government or ministry, against the wishes of the institutions themselves. Magic practitioners may be called up to fight a war, with imprisonment or even death for those who refuse. The ideologies of a religion may be twisted and perverted to serve the purpose of an oppressive government, ruling over its people with the threat of ostracization, public shaming, and eternal damnation.

The rules and guidelines of magic and religion may be re-written into the country's laws, either as they are, or in a cherry-picked or distorted manner. Against the wishes of the institutions, their beliefs may become a weapon of power in a dystopian world.

Individuals within the institutions may, through a deep-rooted belief that their way is the true way, through a corrupt need for power, or through some other motivation, may seek to extend the institutions power beyond its own members. Perhaps the head of a magical society seeks further control, maybe religious leaders seek to 'liberate' and 'save' non-believers by stamping out other beliefs.

Or, perhaps, rebel and vigilante groups adopt religious or magical symbols to further their cause. As an excuse for their actions, or to attach some authority or vindication to them. If the institutions speak out against them, attempting to distance themselves or criticising the behaviour, then maybe the vigilantes simply shout louder.

There are several ways that magic and religion can be used against people, and you only need to look at the history of various religions in our world to see examples of how this has been done. Throw in some magic and sorcery, and you have a great opportunity to create some real danger for your characters, and some violent conflict for your story.

But, it isn't necessarily done on a huge scale. Religion and magic may be used against individuals, or small groups of people. It may be done overtly, boldly and publicly asserting itself, showing off its power, or it may be far more covert. It might gently pick away at the fabric of something, gradually diminishing it without anyone noticing what's happening until it's too late.

Use the following pages to make some notes on the ways in which religion and magic might be used against people in your world.

PERSECUTION AND ERADICATION

Moving in the other direction, away from the weaponisation of religion and magic, let's look at when these institutions are the victims. Either your religious or magical institutions may have been persecuted. They may have been gradually degraded, or they may have been viciously eradicated.

Perhaps a new or imported religion sought to eradicate the old one. Perhaps it outlawed the practices of the old religion, vilifying its practitioners, demonising its gods, pushing it further and further underground. Perhaps its statues were torn down, its buildings seized and repurposed. Maybe its artefacts were destroyed, its texts burnt, its symbols perverted.

It may have been more subtle, with the older practices being adopted into the new religion. Its holidays borrowed and gently changed, its sacred words adapted. Maybe its gods were downgraded to demi-gods, then down to prophets, then to disciples and followers.

Or a religion may have been pushed to the sidelines by its government. Either in preference of a different belief structure, or in pursuit of a secular, non-religious society. It may have been removed from the school curriculum, its believers voted out, its symbols banned in public. It might have been forced behind closed doors, with only the most devout standing stubborn against the ostracization they suffer.

There are many ways to eradicate a belief system, through active removal, through demonisation, or by pushing it to the sidelines to be forgotten.

In the same ways, your magic system may have been persecuted or eradicated altogether. It can suffer the same violent persecution from a new, imported, perhaps stronger form of magic.

There may have been violent clashes between them. Battles. Wars. It may be that, for decades, or centuries, the skies have crackled with their attacks, bleached red, ravaging the land. Maybe the people fight alongside the magical practitioners, or maybe they're fed up of suffering the fallout.

Or the different magical sides may be at a stalemate, existing in a long-held, precarious state of truce. Or it may be a battle of wits, and politics, and snide remarks. It might be a case of dinners, gifts, and promises made to each new monarch, trying to seek their allegiance and approval.

Your magic system may have been pushed to the fringes, leaving nothing more than small, remote pockets of magic. Separated and divided. Their abilities and knowledge greatly reduced, reduced to what their grandparents can remember. It may become little more than myth or legend. It might become just superstitions or tales told by crazy people.

Of course, there is always the possibility of a resurgence. An ancient text discovered, a long-lost talisman appearing. A dead god rising up, a child born with magical abilities that haven't been seen for centuries.

Write some ideas about how your religion or magic system may have been persecuted or eradicated, the state it exists in now, and what kind of future it might bring about.

GROWTH AND DECLINE

The state of your belief and magic systems will not be static, but will change over time. Perhaps over centuries, perhaps just a few generations. But, over time, they will wax and wane in popularity as society evolves.

It may be that the beliefs, rules, and restrictions of a religion or magic system become outdated, and no longer in line with popular opinion. It may be that the practices are long-winded and boring, competing against a world of on-demand entertainment. It may be that, as medical knowledge and technology advance, the need for magic diminishes.

If a religion or magic system refuses, or is unable to adapt to the changes in the world around it, it risks becoming irrelevant, unpopular, even divisive.

In the same way, religions and magic systems can see resurgences and boosts in popularity.

In times of high stress, confusion, or uncertainty, people may turn to the comfort or familiarity of these institutions. Perhaps war has broken out, and the fear encourages people back to religious or magical buildings or sites, asking for help from something they barely believe in. When there's no help from any other source, this can be a common response. You may be writing in a post-apocalyptic world, where people, in their desperation for something to cling to, return to these institutions.

But it's not necessarily a sudden, unexpected shock that might bring about an increase in believers. Your religion or magic system may have preached radical or progressive messages that society wasn't ready for. It may be that, through the evolution of society over the generations, that the wider world has become more aligned with religion and magic, rather than becoming distanced from it.

There may be gradual changes in the political landscape, with each generation becoming more conservative or liberal than their parents. Political parties who are aligned with, or actively part of your religion or magic system may gain traction, finally coming into power. This could mean that laws are changed to reflect the belief structure. That education, gender roles, behaviour norms, all change too. This might be met with anger and resistance, with resignation, or with happiness. It all depends on what's happening in your world.

Immigration and emigration may also play a part. The introduction of new religious and magical cultures might encourage the host society to seek to 'protect' and ring-fence their own culture (even if it's been in decline for generations), or people emigrating might want to take a little piece of their culture with them. They might establish new pockets of followers. They might do so forcefully.

As with every aspect of your world, religion and magic will fall in and out of favour.

They will have a natural ebb and flow, affected by the changes in society, be they rapid or gradual shifts.

Make some notes about the historic or future growth and decline in your religious and magic belief systems. Perhaps one gradually overtakes the other, perhaps they are both fading away, or maybe coming back stronger than before.

INTERACTING WITH THE ENVIRONMENT

You may choose to create a religion or magic system which is very earth-based, working with the elements and the forces of nature. Perhaps you have a religion that worships the sun, reveres the moon, hears God's voice on the wind or in crackles of lightning. Maybe your magic system works with the powers of the earth. Harnessing magnetic energy, collecting weather, using plants or animals.

Even if the link to the environment is less blatant and literal, you may have places of religious or magical importance. Stone circles, mountains, lakes, or forests. Religious buildings might always be built on hills, to bring followers closer to God, or raise them above non-believers. Maybe magic is most powerful at sunrise and sunset, or during the full moon.

Perhaps believers and practitioners turn towards the east, or magnetic north. Maybe their buildings are rooted deep in the earth, with foundations dug deeper than necessary. Perhaps their buildings are carved with images of nature, the pillars supporting the roof made of tree stumps, complete with bark and branches.

The religious or magical cycle of the year, its major festivals, may work with the changing of the seasons, or match the agricultural year. There may be traditions that depend on the weather on a particular holy day, or particular rites that can only be performed during the waxing of the moon.

Even if a religion or magical system appears to be far removed from nature, it may still have its history rooted there. A creation story, telling of how the plants and animals, the sun and the stars, came to be. There may be ancient forests that are said to have been created by magic, or it might be thought to be responsible for the tides.

Even if there isn't a clear, direct link, remember that everything is connected. Everything impacts everything else.

Nature may even be a barrier, or a source of conflict. Maybe magic can't travel through rock, meaning that a mountain village is always protected from sorcery, but cannot practice magic itself. It may be traditional to build religious buildings from a specific stone or timber. One that is rare. Close to extinction.

Perhaps believers are taught that they are trustees of the planet, tasked with its protection. Or maybe that it was God's gift to them, to exploit and use to whatever end they wish for it and themselves.

Whether actively or passively, for better or worse, your religion and magic system will, in some way, have an impact on the environment, and be impacted by it. There is always impact in both directions.

It can be a source of conflict, within the institutions themselves, or against the wider society. It can be a dividing force, or a uniting one. It could lead to the destruction of the planet, or its reconstruction after a disaster.

Write some notes on how your religion and magic system interact with the environment, and what kind of bearing they have upon one another.

CREATING DIVERSITY

Your world is vast, whether you map all of it or not. And in a vast world, there is diversity. There are various cultures, various opinions, various beliefs.

It is likely that, within your whole world, which may well reach beyond the edges of the map you've created, there is more than one religion, and more than one magic system.

It may be that some of the various religions and magic systems are wildly different. Their principles, beliefs, and practices may even directly oppose one another. They might worship different deities, or have different magical abilities using different sources for that magic.

Or, they may be very similar. They might even have common roots. Perhaps they worship the same God, and celebrate the same prophets. Maybe the magic systems are largely the same, but one path has become more theoretical than practical, or one has advanced further, or one has taken magic to a dark place while the moralities of the other won't allow it to follow.

If you want to create a rich, deep, and believable world for your characters, it's good to think about different belief systems that may exist. That your characters might learn about, come into contact with, or possibly wish to convert to.

It can also be a great source of conflict: the cornerstone of every story. This could be conflict on a large scale, with wars against opposing religions or magical institutions. It could be a classic good versus evil story, or a chosen one story, with one group trying to fulfil an ancient prophecy while others try to prevent it. Or the conflict could happen on a much smaller scale, with particular groups, locations, characters. All the way down to an inner conflict where a character wants to follow a different religious or magical path to their parents.

Of course, the various religions and magic systems don't need to be in conflict with each other at all. They might happily exist alongside one another, greatly respecting the right to choose, and to follow one's own faith. But, even when things are harmonious overall, or in appearance, there is often conflict underneath. Either small, isolated pockets of conflict, or a hidden conflict, disguised beneath a falsity of peace.

Perhaps magical academies teach several different magical paths, letting students choose which suits them best. Meanwhile, there is vicious rivalry between the students themselves, viewing certain magical paths as better, stronger, or more noble than others.

Maybe various religions live alongside one another relatively peacefully. Perhaps they hold inter-faith meetings and services, or have a joint council. But underneath, vigilante groups are carrying out their own form of violent justice, punishing those who follow the 'wrong' faith.

You might want to map out different religions and magical systems as deeply as each other, making the conflicts and relations between them the crux of your story. Alternatively, you may simply create a rough sketch of other belief systems, only ever mentioning them in passing. Create them as much or as little as your story needs you to. As much as your readers need it.

MONOPOLIES

It may be the case that your religion or magic systems requires its members to remain exclusive, and not follow principles or practices from other belief structures. They may require complete and singular devotion.

The strictness of this rule would be up to you. Perhaps members of your religion are ostracised and branded as 'sinners' for trying out a meditation from another religion, or for befriending and associating with its followers. Maybe they are expected to distance themselves from family members who are non-believers. Or, it may be a generalised, accepted norm to remain devout. That no one's actions are watched or questioned, and no shame is placed on them for stepping over the border of their faith.

Likewise, it might be that a curious student of one magic system might be cast out, or violently punished, for reading a book about another system, or for picking up one of their magical tools. Perhaps students are expected to choose their path at a young age, and knowledge of any other magical route is kept from them. Perhaps their path isn't even a choice they are given.

On the other hand, your religion and magic system might allow, or even encourage, followers to try out different things. To read and learn widely, and find their own way, even if they borrow from different belief structures. It may be a cultural norm in your world, for people to mix religions and magic systems, and to belong, jointly, to more than one.

Maybe there are academies and places of worship designed to allow for these crossovers.

When you're thinking about how monopolistic your institutions are, think about the kind of punishments people may suffer for stepping outside their institution. Everything from tuts and shaking heads, gossip, ostracisation, all the way up to banishment, excommunication, or even corporal and capital punishments. Also consider what might lead someone to risk these things.

If crossover is allowed, consider how this works in day-to-day life. Consider religions and magic systems that are similar and closely aligned, versus those that seem like polar opposites.

Again, this offers another opportunity for conflict; from wide-reaching conflict, to personal, inner conflict.

Make some notes about how monopolistic your religions and magic systems are, and what this means for their followers. Because that's what's important; how it affects your characters. They're the reason your readers keep reading.

EXCLUSIVITY AND INCLUSION

We've now reached the final prompt in the Fitting into Society section, so you will now have a good idea of how your religions and magic systems interact with your wider society. How they have effected the world around them, and how that world has effected them.

In this prompt, we'll look at access to religion and magic, and who is, or isn't allowed to practice it.

It may be that your religion is open to everyone. It may be that anyone can enter your religious buildings, without judgement or prejudice, and worship there, and be included. However, it may be that certain buildings, or areas of buildings, are segregated; keeping one portion of followers away from others. This division may be based on anything: age, gender, wealth, parentage, race, physical ability, role within the religion, past misdemeanours. Anything you choose.

Perhaps only certain people are able to read the ancient texts. Maybe only some people can be included in certain rites and rituals. Maybe particular followers can't access services, and are left in side rooms, listening on speakers, or watching on screens. Maybe some people are considered 'unclean' or 'unworthy', for whatever reason you wish to place upon them.

It may be that some people aren't worthy, or high enough, to have direct access to the deity, or to religious artefacts, or locations. It may be that you have to inherit that privilege, or pay for it.

Likewise, it may be that everyone in your world is capable of practising magic. However, magical education may only be accessible by a few. Access to books, fighting arenas, sorcery tools, whatever, is restricted. Again, you can choose the manner of these restrictions, and, of course, the fallout of the inequality.

It might be that certain parts of society are banned, by law, from practising magic, or owning certain artefacts or texts. Maybe one form of magic is considered more noble than another, and its secrets are closely guarded. Again, the access key to the inner sanctum is up to you. Perhaps only women can practice magic, or only rich boys can enter the academy. Maybe you had to have been born under a full moon, or receive a blessing from a magical leader.

Are there ways that people can better their position? Gain access to places that were previously denied to them? Or are their fortunes set the moment they're born?

You can make your religions and magical institutions as fair or unfair as you choose. Just remember, always, to bring it back to the level of your characters. How does it affect them? How do they feel about it? And what are they going to do about it?

NAMES, TITLES, AND SPECIALIST TERMS

We're now moving into the Nuts and Bolts section, and this is the part I've been waiting for! This is where we get to really have some fun.

Now, when you're working on the nuts and bolts of your religions and magic systems, you can use everything you have in your creative arsenal. You can make up crazy things, beautiful things, amazing things. This is where you can get your readers to say "wow" and "that's so cool" and maybe even "this author is the cleverest, most creative author I've ever known, and I shall buy every book they ever write."

If you're making your way through this workbook in order, you will have already thought about how your religions and magic systems fit into your wider world. As you work through the nuts and bolts, you may wish to look back at your notes from the previous section, or add to them, or even change them. Because it's really important that both sections work together. You can make up some of the weirdest and wildest things you can imagine, but for them to be believable, for your reader to feel immersed in a world that feels solid and real, it needs to make sense in your world. Let me say that again: it needs to make sense in your world.

Just as you want your characters to be realistic, believable and relatable, so too, you want your world to be. You want your readers to walk in your world, to smell the smells, and touch the fabric of it. You want them to, when they finish reading, feel the jolt of returning to the real world (and, perhaps, a little bit of disappointment too!) To do that, everything in your world should fit together seamlessly. Like it has always been there. Like it grew there. Like the world wouldn't be the same without it. You don't want to bolt things on randomly, or force things into spaces where they don't fit. Your readers will feel the disconnect, which is not something you want them to feel.

And so, let's kick off with names, titles, and specialist terms.

The big one, of course, is the name of your religion or magic system. It might be named after the founder, or another important leader. It might be named after a central aspect or principle. Your magic system might be named after the source of its power, or your religion might be named after its deity, or a collective name for several deities.

This is also something that you can backwards engineer. You can pick a name, at random if you like, and then figure out what significance it might have. There are loads of random name and word generators online, including ones where you can pick specific themes or sounds for the words it produces. A simple internet search will offer up many, but I regularly use Seventh Sanctum (seventhsanctum.com) and Cult of Squid (squid.org/rpg-random-generator).

There are all sorts of other things that you might like to name, such as different denominations, or sub-groups, artefacts, texts. You may wish to create magical words, or special words recited during ceremonies. You might want to name your buildings, your leadership ranks, your students, or those who have graduated to the next stage. The world really in your naming oyster.

One thing to always bear in mind is your reader's learning curve. For every specialist term, your reader's learning curve gets a tiny bit steeper. You will need to make the meaning of these words obvious through the context in which you're using them. And the more specialist words you use, the more frequently they appear, the more work you're asking your reader to do.

Getting the balance right isn't always easy. It is something that you learn through experience (both of reading and writing), and something that you can test out with beta readers. You can find more information about easing your reader's learning curve at the back of this book, in A Word on Info Dumping and Learning Curves.

If you would really like to have some fun, you can bring in slang terms, or swear words, or insults. They can be great for adding more cultural flavour and colour to your world, as long as, once again, you're making the context clear enough for your readers to decipher.

Many writers choose to include a glossary in their books, listing all of the specialist terms and their definitions. If you decide to include one, it should sit as an optional extra, a bit of fun for your readers. It shouldn't be an essential part of their understanding of the world. You don't want to have your readers flicking back and forth to the glossary as a matter of necessity. Every time they're forced to that glossary, you're kicking them out of the immersion of your story. Use your story, your worldbuilding, and your characters to make the meaning clear on all of your specialist terms.

Use the spaces below to begin creating a glossary for yourself. This is something you're likely to keep coming back and adding to, as you work your way through the other prompts in this book. Have fun with it, and go wild. You can always reign it back in, and choose not to include them all.

SYMBOLS

Symbols and insignias can be used to identify followers of a particular religion or magic system to one another. This might be a public, widely recognised symbol, or it may be a secret one, known only by those permitted to bear it.

Symbols can be powerful things. They can encourage hope, devotion, and loyalty. They can offer a sense of belonging and comradeship. Equally, they can encourage devotion or obedience through fear. They can remind someone of their position, or of who owns them. They can be used for hatred, oppression, and exclusion.

Remember that symbols can mean one thing to one person, and something quite different to another. Also, symbols can change their meaning over time. They can be reclaimed by an oppressed people, turned into a sign of courage, revolution, revenge.

The power of a symbol can be metaphorical or literal. A magical symbol could be a spell in itself; a place where magic originates, or a protection from magical attacks. They could be used to summon gods or demons, as a communication device, a transporter, or a location marker. There are so many different ways in which symbols can be used.

You can create symbols by looking at the important parts of your religions or magic systems, and incorporating them into the design. Think about the message you wish the symbol to portray; what your characters should feel when they see it. This is another thing that you can backwards engineer: creating a symbol, and then working out how it fits in.

Consider making symbols for different purposes. One for public use, one for private. One to encourage hope, one to encourage unquestioning obedience. Think about the kind of power that symbol might contain, and who has the knowledge to use it.

Perhaps the original meanings, or powers, of a symbol have been forgotten, lost, or confused over time. Perhaps purposefully perverted or manipulated. Which symbols are people hoarding to themselves? Which are being hidden to protect the world, and who gets to decide that?

Which secret societies are operating, and how do they recognise one another? Perhaps a seemingly meaningless badge, a small tattoo, or a pattern shaved into hair.

What happens if someone stumbles upon a symbol they don't understand? What happens if they unleash something they didn't mean to? Does anyone know the symbol that locks it back up again?

Have fun with creating your symbols, but, as ever, always keep thinking about the impact on the characters. How they use them, how they feel about them, how they want to change them.

FOUNDERS

If you're writing about a newly established religion or magic system (or a new offshoot of an older one), it may well be that the founder is still alive and well, and actively leading their movement.

What kind of leader are they? And how did they come to such a position? Perhaps they are happy with what they've created, or perhaps it turned into something they didn't like, into something they hadn't intended, and they've distanced themselves from it. Maybe they never meant to lead a movement at all. Maybe they were seeking their own truth and, despite their efforts at living a reclusive life, they are hounded and harassed by people seeking leadership and instruction.

On the other hand, your religions and magic systems may be older—as ancient as the world itself, or older still—and the founders long dead. This is where you get to play a little. After all, the centuries that have passed have granted their own artistic licence to the stories, so why shouldn't you?

There may well be different founding stories: one that exists as legend, one that exists as the accepted truth. There may be stories of deities or mythical beings that passed the knowledge to humans, or there may be a story of a human who somehow discovered the true faith, the true path. A human who discovered the secret to it all.

These stories are likely to have changed over time, even if the contemporary believers have complete faith that it is the absolute truth as it happened. Religions or magical institutions may have split over different versions of these stories, creating different branches and sub-groups.

Perhaps the institutions are named after their founders, perhaps the founders' names are long forgotten. Perhaps the truth has been purposefully lost, or wiped from record, or twisted and transformed.

The founders may be revered and worshipped, they may be very present in the day-to-day practices of their followers. Or they may be merely a historical footnote. A single lesson in the curriculum. A brief mention in some ancient text.

But do remember, that they were a person, or persons, with lives and families and hopes and dreams. With flaws and pretences and all the human attributes. And they have had an impact on the way your religions and magical institutions are run, whether they're credited for it or not.

FOREMOST PRINCIPLES

Quite often, belief structures can be boiled down to a small set of instructions, rules, or guidelines. Of course, this is a simplification of the institution as a whole, but, for this prompt, it's that rulebook that we want to look at.

You may be able to sum up the foremost principles in one simple guideline. Just one, that encompasses the kind of attitude followers are encouraged to take. Or, it may be more than one. A set. Three. Five. Ten. Eighty-six. Whatever works for your institution.

You may wish to make your principles clear and specific. Don't do this, don't do that, don't do the other. You may wish them to be more broad. Be good. Be kind. Be honest.

When you're thinking about these rules, think about the image the institution wants to project. Does it want people to view it as merciful? As peace-loving? As powerful and formidable? The image it seeks to project, of course, may be nothing more than a ruse. A bit of clever PR. But its foremost principles will be part of that.

Also think about where these guidelines have come from. The founders? Straight from the mouth of a deity? Perhaps they're more recent, put in place by leaders, or forced upon an institution by the government. Perhaps, over the years, changes in society have forced these rules to be adapted. Perhaps they became outdated, offensive, dangerous, in the changing society they existed in.

It may be that these principles have had to be added to, in order to keep up with a changing world. It may be that they've been adapted to change the public image of an institution, or adapted in times of great social upheaval. For example, rules about not using magic as a weapon may have been overruled during a time of war. Principles about the role of women may have been adapted when fertility rates plummeted.

These foremost principles can leave these institutions at odds with the world. It could see them being left behind, or steaming ahead. It could see them persecuted or attacked, or it could require the government or the army to stand against them.

At a more personal level, these principles could cause conflict between neighbours, friends, families. They could be the source of an internal, moral struggle. They could be a barrier between your protagonist and their goal.

So, when you're listing the foremost principles for your religious and magical institutions, think about how they might affect the wider society, those within the institution, and individual characters themselves. Think about how they might help or hinder your protagonist, or how your protagonist might seek to rewrite them.

CONSEQUENCES AND LIMITATIONS

When you're building a magic system, consequences and limitations are really important. If your magic is limitless and all-powerful, if nothing bad ever happens from using it, then your protagonist can get anything they want, whenever they want it. The story starts and finishes on page one as they magic up everything they ever desire from life. There's no barriers to getting it, no struggle, no try/fail cycles, no journey, and no character development.

If you'd like your story to last a little bit longer than a single page, then you need conflict, and that comes in the form of barriers: things that stop your protagonist from achieving their goal.

For example, imagine your main character's overall goal in your story is to reach a sanctuary and start a new life away from the post-apocalyptic, dystopian hell they're living in. If they flick a magic wand, and arrive there just like that, with nothing to stop them, then you have no story.

Now, it may well be that a flick of a magic wand will get them there. But they may need to retrieve that magic wand from beneath the foot of a mighty, and very deadly, dragon. Suddenly, you have barriers and conflicts, because you've placed a limitation on your magic system: that wands are rare, and difficult to get hold of. You see, the magic itself may be limitless, but the means of making that magic are not.

It may also be the case that the magic is limitless, wands are as common as raindrops, but, there's a 75% chance that the user of the magic will simply blow off their own arm in the process. Consequences. And if your main character is the sole earner in their family, with their father deceased, and their increasingly sick mother caring for their dying sister, then the potential loss of an arm is a big decision to make.

And so, in order to create conflict and struggle, your magic system needs consequences, or limitations, or both.

With a magic system, it's simple to see the need for these things, and ways in which to create them. But what about placing similar problems into your religions?

This largely comes down to whether your deities are listening, and how willing they are to intervene. If your deities are uninterested in the affairs of mankind, or forbidden from intervening, long-dead, or somewhat sadistic, you have a limitation in your religion. If their intervention requires a human sacrifice, or a balancing out of the help they give in some unexpected, often cruel manner, then you have consequences.

Limitations and consequences are the perfect tool for increasing tension in your story and ramping up the stakes for your characters. Don't be scared to be mean; that's when your characters really get to shine. And this section is so essential to the success of your story, be sure to give it due attention.

And remember, it doesn't need to be your actual magic or religion itself that has limits and consequences. It could be that a character lacks knowledge or ability, and has no one to teach them, or that the knowledge was lost or forgotten centuries ago. Perhaps the specific words needed, or the insignias, or the raw materials are long-lost or extinct. Perhaps your character needs to use a compromise, a near-enough-but-not-quite element that gives unpredictable results.

Perhaps it needs specific weather conditions on specific dates. Perhaps it takes weeks or months of preparation, or requires the practitioner to bleed out almost to the point of death.

It could be that the limitations and consequences have been placed there by the government, that certain spells or rituals have been outlawed. Perhaps only certain people are able to use them. Maybe the use of magic alerts the authorities to your location, or alerts an enemy. Maybe the use of magic, even in a life-or-death situation could mean lifelong incarceration or a death penalty.

And always be thinking about how you can bring this back to your world and the main themes of your story. If it's an environmental story, make the environment a limitation. If it's a feminist story, make gender the limitation. If it's romance, then love. Tie the limitations and consequences to your antagonist, be that a single person, a government, or the world itself. Everything needs to be linked.

There are so many ways in which you can place barriers between your main character and their goals using limitations and consequences. You can raise the stakes and force them to make an impossible choice. You can hit them with struggle after struggle, before standing them back up for more. You can abandon them to self pity, and strip them of their belief in anything.

After all, even genies come with small print: no wishing for wishes, remember?

HOW PRESENT IS GOD?

This isn't just a question for the sake of your religions. Magic systems are equally able to have deities, or to be tightly tied to a religion.

Your deities may be very present in the day-to-day lives of humans. They may walk among them, live among them, fall in love with them and have children together. They may do this in disguise, or with everyone knowing exactly who and what they are. They might exist like celebrities, crowded everywhere they go by people trying to get close. On the other hand, they might be vilified, shunned, or hated, and find themselves as unwelcome guests in every town.

Deities may only have direct contact with people through intermediaries. Angels, demons, fae, folk, spirits, ghosts, shadows, whatever you choose to call them. They may act as mouthpieces and conduits, or they may have been given authority to act on their own judgement, only disturbing the deities in an emergency. They might have gone rogue, hungry for power, and overstepping their roles.

The deities might have very little to do with humans. They might not even be watching or listening anymore. Maybe people have forgotten their names, and are unable to call on them.

The deities may even be long-dead, whether people know it or not. They may have taken a vow not to intervene, or they may have made an agreement with humans to leave them to get on with it.

Perhaps your deities are spiteful and jealous. Maybe they are indifferent and detached. Perhaps they are watchful, but silent.

How present your deities are will impact the way religions and magic systems work. It will impact people's faith, and the way they act regarding their faith. It will impact the kind of things they ask for, and how often they ask. It will impact in what they are willing to do in return.

After all, once a subject is aware that they are being observed, their behaviour automatically changes.

Think also about what might happen if a previously invisible deity suddenly becomes very, very present. Or, if a previously active deity suddenly disappears.

CREATION STORIES

Everything starts somewhere. At some point, your world came into existence. There may have been something before it, just darkness perhaps, or the birth of your world may have been the dawn of time. Of everything.

Such a huge occasion deserves a few stories about it, right? A few myths and legends.

Creation stories can exist for both your religions and magic systems. They may be similar, they may be wildly different. What they are likely to be is awe-inspiring. It's good for business.

Creation stories aren't stories of accidental happenings. They aren't stories of science or logic or random reactions between chemicals. They are stories of purpose and design. They are stories of an all-encompassing power, a power that created a world for your people. A power that they owe their thanks to. For everything. For all time.

Of course, the exception to this (there's always one, isn't there?) would be if you had a belief structure or magic system deeply rooted in science, or an atheistic one. That's absolutely for you to play with.

Maybe your creation story is about an author, who had an idea, and picked up their pen!

As with everything, think about how this creation story links into your religions and magic systems. Think about how it serves their purposes, and puts across the message they want to portray. What lesson it teaches. What values and norms of behaviour it promotes. What prejudices.

Think about how it fits into the wider world, into the laws of nature (sunrise, sunset, the phases of the moon, etc), and into the rules mankind has created (money, time, calendars, class structures, etc.) Consider how a creation story might be used to vindicate and uphold these man-made constructs, as if they weren't made by mankind at all, but by God. Consider how a creation story might fit with the laws of nature, in a way that gives credence and plausibility to it. In a way that makes it harder to deny or dismiss as fiction.

Think about how creation stories may have been altered and adapted over time, to suit the changing needs and focus of these institutions. How they might be used to raise some people up, while oppressing others.

MYTHS, LEGENDS, AND SUPERSTITIONS

While we're on the subject of stories, let's look at some even more fantastical ones. All the myths, legends, and superstitions that surround your religions and magic systems.

There will be stories that have started within the institutions themselves. Perhaps tales of great battles, impossible heroes, and staggering miracles. Stories that are designed to impress, to entice, maybe to inspire fear. Again, it all depends on the kind of impression your institution wants to project. What serves their purposes?

There may also be stories that comes from outside of the institutions, stories they have less control over. These might be less favourable stories; stories of great defeats, of genocide and cruelty, of the death of their deity.

It might be that members of your religions and magic systems are very superstitious people. They might have rituals and habits designed to protect them from bad fortune or curses. They might have symbols and talismans to keep them safe. There might be localised customs as well as widespread ones.

Perhaps a certain religious building has a grove above its door, worn smooth from everyone entering touching it, in a ritual believed to lay a blessing on them. Maybe one magical academy has a circle of iron sewn into their cloaks after a past student was saved from attack by something similar. There may even be customs that are done simply because they always have been, long after anyone remembers why.

These stories, these rituals and habits, may make people the source of ridicule. They may be thought of as simpletons, or even heretics for the superstitions they cling onto. It might cause a certain section of believers to break away, and create their own sub-group.

Think about where these stories have come from, and what part they have played in history. Think about what part they play in the present, and how they might affect the future. Keep tying them back to everything else you've created, and, most importantly, to your characters.

Maybe your protagonist sets out to debunk a legend that has become a tool for oppression. Maybe they're looking to prove one that could enlighten the world and make it a better place. Perhaps they uncover a secret, and agonise over the decision to reveal it. Perhaps ignorance is the bliss society needs.

Maybe your protagonist wants to become a legend, or create a new one. Maybe they accidentally become one, falling into a hero role they never wanted. Perhaps a belief in a superstition is a barrier to them reaching their goal, and they have to overcome years of ingrained beliefs and practices. Perhaps they dismiss a superstition as nonsense, only to fall foul of its curse.

BUILDINGS

Buildings are much more than simple bricks and mortar. They can be sanctuaries or prisons. They can mean belonging or exclusion. You can be locked inside them, or locked out of them. They can stand as monuments, as dedications, as ostentatious displays of sanctimony and superiority. They can be warnings; stark reminders of what happens to those who step out of line.

They can have gruesome histories that taint the walls. They can be reminders of revolution, or war, or a great renaissance. They can be adored, protected, or destroyed.

They can stand for centuries, they can be erected for a single event, or designed to wash away with the next rainstorm.

Perhaps buildings have been erected on other sacred sites, in an effort to erase that part of the world's history. Maybe buildings have been appropriated and converted. Maybe buildings have been built to outshine another, or to divert attention from a shameful past.

When thinking about your religious and magical buildings and spaces, think about their purpose; both practical and metaphorical. Do they need to be made of wood for the magic to work, or made from iron-lined rock to contain it? Are they built tall, bringing followers closer to their deities? Are they hidden below ground, or in the back rooms of grimy diners, or in the spaces between the walls of houses?

Do they stand as grand monuments of faith and devotion, or are they built to reflect the fleetingness of life; to show that nothing lasts forever? Your spaces might not be buildings at all, but outside spaces that become places of pilgrimage. A clearing in a forest, a mountain, a lake.

Also consider who has commissioned and paid for these buildings. And, who built them? Highly paid architects? Low-paid manual workers? Volunteers? Slaves?

What scars do these buildings carry? Perhaps all of their statues have had the faces scraped away. Maybe murals have been painted over. Maybe the walls are pock-marked with bullet holes or striped with sword blows. Perhaps blood decorates the walls, and skulls are piled at the altar, reminding followers of the persecution their forebears suffered and endured.

Consider who is allowed into these buildings, and who is excluded. Or how people are segregated inside. Who gets the front seats? Who is hidden from sight? Do people go to see, or to be seen? Perhaps there are rooms that no one has ever seen, or spaces that have been sealed shut for centuries.

There may be places that people dare not go. Haunted places, cursed places, or places that perpetuate such stories to protect the secrets hidden there. Are buildings restricted or fortified to keep people out, or to keep something in?

SACRED AND HISTORIC ARTEFACTS

Here's another fun section for you, where you can really let your imagination run wild. Every good religion needs sacred artefacts, and every good magic system needs magical objects, whether they really exist, or only exist in stories and legends.

Think about the place these artefacts have in your institutions. Their purpose, their power, their history. Why are these particular artefacts held sacred over others?

Consider how and where they are stored, and who has access to them. Perhaps they are only brought out once a year, for a particular event. Perhaps they are present at specific rites and rituals. Maybe they are brought out for the equinox, or the new moon, or to celebrate births or marriages. Maybe they are never brought out at all, but kept secure, or hidden. They might be used every single day, or take pride of place in people's homes. Just because they are sacred or historic, doesn't mean that they are rarely used. They may be a deeply ingrained part of believers' everyday lives.

Think about the stories of the artefacts themselves. Where did they come from? Who made them? How did they become sacred? Perhaps they once belonged to a religious leader or founder. Perhaps they were a gift from God. Maybe they hold the secret to untold magical powers, or contain the soul of an evil entity.

Perhaps there are artefacts that were lost or stolen long ago. Perhaps not everyone believes they actually existed. What would happen if they were suddenly uncovered? What secrets might be uncovered with them? It might be enough to topple a leader, or the entire institution itself. Perhaps there are people with a vested interest in that item staying lost.

You may have artefacts that, while they are still brought out for rituals, the actual purpose of them has been long forgotten. Artefacts that, at some point, may have been practical, might now be nothing more than symbolic. Perhaps the knowledge of how to use them has been lost, or they have been broken at some point. Maybe their use has been confused, and they're used improperly. What might happen if someone, without the knowledge of how to wield them, picks them up? What if a novice somehow awakens a power in them that has been dormant for centuries?

There may be artefacts that have been confiscated or banned. They might be dangerous, either in their actual power, or in the ideas or history they represent. An institution might have to disassociate itself from a certain artefact, locking it away, or destroying it.

When creating your sacred and historic artefacts, keep in mind everything you know about the institution and its place in society. What image do they want to project? How does this differ to what happens behind closed doors?

Stick to the theme of your institutions: whether they're earth-based, work with spirits, project an image of violence, or are viewed as peace-loving. How do these artefacts reflect those themes and ideals, or how do they directly oppose them?

EVERYDAY OBJECTS

Alongside the sacred objects, your institutions will also have everyday objects that they use. That, while they are an ingrained part of the religions and magic systems, they are not rare, or old, or expensive, or precious. They may be precious to that person's faith, or have sentimental value, or it may be something throwaway, or something they can easily replace.

There can be everyday objects that followers keep and use in their homes, there can be objects that they wear, or carry on them, or objects used in religious and magical buildings and academies.

You might consider things like jewellery and clothing, pipes for smoking and herbs or tobacco. Things like traditional food and drink, drinking vessels, candles and incense, chalk, charcoal, or salt.

You may also have altar items; altar cloths, statuettes, paintings, bells, balls, wands, candlesticks. You might have items used for healing, or for divination, such as runes, cards, crystals, dowsing rods, mirrors. Perhaps books and pens, talismans, banners, flags, and pennants, or weapons, or items that represent weapons.

Some of these items might be passed down through the family; from father to son, or mother to daughter. They might be gifts for important milestones: births, naming ceremonies, coming of age, graduations, marriages, deaths.

They might be given as achievements, as a person moves up through the ranks of a religion or magic system.

You may have items that are present in every home, or in every institution's building, that are barely glanced at. They're so everyday, that people don't even notice them. Until they disappear. Or change.

As with the sacred items, think about *why* these objects are there. What purpose do they have? What do they represent? What makes them part of one religion or magical system, and not part of another?

There may be items that have fallen out of favour, and are no longer popular. There may be items that have only recently started being used. There may be things that are considered old-fashioned, and users of them are ridiculed or pitied. Perhaps your characters can't afford the updated versions, or are otherwise prevented from owning them.

Think about the importance they have to your characters. Are your characters proud of a particular object, wearing it prominently as a mark of honour? Are they ashamed, or afraid of the repercussions, and hide it away?

IMPORTANT TEXTS

Important texts can come in many different forms. They might be mass-produced as books, with ancient and original versions either long-lost, or locked away for safety. They may only exist in those original forms, and not be widely available to followers. They may be bound books, loose sheets, scrolls, stone tablets, anything.

There may be several different important texts, such as spell books, prayer books, poetry books, rule books, and instructions for rites and rituals. They might be literal instructions, or they might be more metaphorical and reflective. These may have been written by leaders, prophets, ordinary followers, or come from the mouths of the deities themselves.

Their creation might be mentioned in myths and legends, or even in the original creation stories.

They might be used in rites and rituals, they might be read everyday, they might be the source of years of study, they might still be going through translation.

Once again, it's important to think about their position within your institutions. How they suit the needs of that institution. Do they promote obedience and devotion? Do they promote hierarchy, and the importance of knowing one's place? Are they used to perpetuate prejudice, oppression, and exclusion?

Consider the effect these texts, and the messages within them, might have on your characters. Are they hiding the truth about themselves because they go against the narrative? Are they struggling with contradictions and hypocrisies within the texts? Is there conflict where modern society disagrees with rules in the texts?

Look at the history of these texts. Not just who wrote them, but who has translated them over time. Who is able to read the original documents? Who knows whether they've been accurately and truthfully translated or reproduced?

Consider what might happen if a new text were to be discovered, or missing pages from a text. Perhaps you have texts that are indecipherable; what would happen if someone was finally able to read them?

RITES AND RITUALS

Rites and rituals are a really important part of religions and magic systems. They are used to offer a sense of importance and reverence, of practicality and relevance, of togetherness and community. They can be used to mark achievements; big life milestones, or graduating from one level to another. They can be the way to make the magic work, or to speak to God. They can also be used to show off wealth and power, to bask in one's own importance, or as a show of influence and control.

You can bring out your sacred and historic artefacts, as well as the everyday objects, and deck the buildings out with symbols. You can bring in all of the names, titles, and specialist terms, read from ancient texts, and put out your entire worldbuilding arsenal for your readers.

Think about what the rites and rituals are marking: an anniversary for the institution, a historic event, a founder's birthday. It might be to swear in a new leader, or to celebrate someone graduating to the next level. It might be a personal event; a naming ceremony, coming of age, marriage, death.

Consider the theme of the event; is it a joyous celebration, a sombre remembrance, a reverent and serious event, or a mourning? Is there music or dancing? Food? Is the building decorated? Consider how many people attend, and who attends.

It might be that only certain people are allowed to attend particular rites and rituals. Based on their position in the institution, their ability, their family lineage. They may need to buy their way in with donations, or have completed a number of tasks. Maybe only men or women can attend, or children, even.

You can add as much drama to these events as you wish, ramping up the dramatics, either to impress and amaze your readers, or to push past that point to ridicule and parody. It depends on how your characters feel about it, and how you want your readers to feel. You can use these moments to change your readers' view of an institution; to transform a terrifying one into pompous and laughable, to transform a trivial one into serious and deep-thinking.

You can add colour and flavour to your institutions with ritualistic words and actions. But make them mean something; don't add things for the sake of adding them. Give them weight, and reason, and importance, by tying them to everything you've already decided about your institutions. And remember to tie them to your characters.

Maybe this is an event your protagonist has been looking forward to, perhaps they have been dreading it. Maybe they're wrestling with inner conflict: happy to see their friend graduating, but jealous that they're being left behind. Or happy to see their brother come of age, but sad that he'll be going away for the next two years. Perhaps they can't understand a ritual, as it is spoken in a language they have no knowledge of.

Maybe they sneak into a ritual they're not allowed to attend, only to discover a horrifying truth. Perhaps they skip out on a ritual, and are prevented from moving to the next stage. Maybe they discover they were left off the invite list for a rite their best friend attended, and kept secret from them.

While rites and rituals are a great tool for adding more intrigue and excitement to your institutions, be sure to hook them up to your story and, most importantly, your characters and their journeys.

FESTIVALS

Right, let's get this party started, shall we? Festivals are a fun and exciting way to add some cultural flavour to your worldbuilding. There are so many things that you can show readers about your world through festivals and celebrations.

You can show them food and drink, entertainment, leisure. You can introduce visitors from other countries and cultures, importing their food, drink, and entertainment. You can use this to highlight the differences or similarities, or to cause conflict, or to derail your character's journey. It might be your protagonist's first experience of diversity, or of a particular culture. It could mark the beginning of their journey.

You can also explore things like work versus leisure. Who is allowed to attend the festival? Who is granted time away from their job? Who is barred from attending? Perhaps children aren't allowed to go, or unmarried women, or non-magical people.

You an also show the important points in your world's calendar. What do the festivals represent, what are they celebrating? The changing seasons, a successful harvest, the equinox or solstice. Perhaps it's a significant anniversary: the founding of the town, the vanquishing of a dragon, a battle victory, the death of the last witch (at least, they think it was the last!)

Festivals needn't always be related to your religions or magic systems. They may be secular festivals that these institutions either involve themselves in, or decry and shun. Perhaps they started out as religious or magical events, and they've been hijacked, with the original meaning pushed aside in favour of commercialism or debauchery. Perhaps your religions and magic systems are trying to reclaim the events, or set up their own in direct competition.

Festivals can be divisive, and cause conflict. They can highlight division, or prejudice and inequality in your world. They might be celebrating a dark part of your world's history, that many feel shouldn't be celebrated and glamourised at all. There may be festivals that have been outlawed altogether, or only take place in secret, out in the forest, the mountains, or behind closed doors.

Festivals might bring trouble with them; fights and arguments. Crime. Protests. Litter and damage. Perhaps the townspeople are on their last warning, holding the festival under threat of closure. Maybe there are clashes between the people and the authorities.

There may be festivals that have become unpopular, with only the most devout followers still attending. Or there may be festivals that have doubled or tripled in size over the years.

Also, think about what happens the morning after. Are people expected to go straight back to work? Who cleans up the mess? Maybe the festivals last for a whole weekend, or a week, or even longer. Perhaps just unofficially, by those determined to extend the festivities themselves.

HIERARCHY AND ELECTION

Within your institutions, there are most likely people holding different ranks. There is most likely a hierarchy. Of course, your institution might have no leaders. Perhaps every single person has an equal vote and equal voice. But, even so, they're likely to have particular roles within that.

Mapping out the leadership of your institution is just like creating the structure of your government, or making a family tree. There will be different ranks, different levels, each with their own amount of power and responsibility. There may be only one person on each level, changing only when that person dies or steps down. Or there may be levels with several representatives.

You can have a bit of fun naming those levels, and the roles within them. Because naming things is fun. Just have a think, once again, about the image your institution wants to portray. Perhaps the leader is known as a 'monarch' to give them an image of ultimate power. Perhaps the leaders are known as 'voices' or 'vessels' who speak for the people they represent. Maybe they're called 'officers' or 'linemen' or 'booters', giving them an air of authority. Maybe they're called 'bearers', to represent that the weight of responsibility is a burden rather than an elevated, privileged position. It all depends on the message you want to convey about them, and the role they play.

Also consider how they rise to that position. Are the roles inherited, passed down through powerful families? Are they democratically elected, or less-than-democratically elected? Are they voted in by their peers, helped along by money slipped into some pockets? Perhaps they need to win a competition of intelligence, strength, obedience, or magical ability. Maybe something they are born with makes them a more likely candidate than someone else. Maybe they have to earn the position, either honestly, or less so.

Think about who is able to stand for election, and who is allowed to vote. If certain groups of people are barred from either activity, then they will not have a voice in the leadership circle. They won't have people who truly understand their lives, their needs, their struggles. It may be that your leadership is solely made up of white, upper-class men, or mothers, or of the most elite sorcerers, or the most talented shape-shifters. How does that impact on the decisions they make? How does it impact the demographics of people who are not represented?

Consider the roles that each leadership level take on. What responsibilities they have, and what level of power. Are their votes equal, or do their decisions need to pass through a higher authority before getting the go-ahead? Maybe the general members of the institution have the final vote, either granting or declining the proposals their leaders put to them.

Think about abuses of power, and corruption that might exist within the hierarchy. Consider the prejudice, and who might be kept out of decisions, even though they have a right to be included. Think about who might cause upset if they were to be unexpectedly voted in, and what kind of upset they might cause. Think about what might happen if the people needed to revolt against their leadership; to topple and replace it.

UNIFORMS AND CLOTHING

When we look at uniforms and clothing, always keep in mind that, what people choose *not* to wear, can be just as important as what they *do* choose to wear.

Your institution may have a certain uniform that its members are required to wear. This may be anything from a singular article, to a full outfit. It may be reserved for special occasions, or each time they enter a sacred building, or every single day.

It might be worn as a matter of pride, as a badge of honour. It might be hidden away, or concealed so that only other members of the institution recognise it. Or it might be worn through a legal requirement to mark them out, as a mark of shame.

There may be uniforms that are only worn by those in a position of leadership, with different designs or colours to distinguish the different ranks.

They might wear certain clothes for the sake of practicality. Perhaps their magic requires use of fire, so they only wear short sleeves. Maybe it requires gymnastics, and they wear loose, or stretchy clothes. Perhaps rituals dictate that followers are on their knees throughout, and padded sections are sewn into the knees of their trousers. Maybe it is traditional that people cover their faces, or their hands, or their necks, when meeting their God. Maybe they're supposed to be naked.

In the absence of a specific uniform or specialist clothing, there might still be codes of practice, and expected norms when it comes to clothing. Perhaps women are expected to wear skirts of a certain length, and men are expected to wear ties. Maybe clothes should be modest, or figure-hugging, or of a particular colour. Maybe beards are traditional, or long hair, or shaved heads. Perhaps there is specific jewellery, or jewellery might be forbidden.

There may be certain tattoos that followers either like to get, or are required to. Perhaps they receive scars or marks in their skin to show their devotion and membership.

Remember, what they choose *not* to wear is just as important, and they might avoid certain colours that are synonymous with rival institutions. They might avoid certain brands or manufacturers because they aren't in-line with their beliefs. There may be particular fabrics and fibres that they avoid because of their beliefs. Or it might be certain styles of clothes they avoid. They might always need to show their wrists, or cover their feet.

As ever, keep bringing it back to the roots of the beliefs. Those core principles. And keep bringing it back to the characters. How do they feel about their clothes? Does it make them feel like they belong to something bigger than themselves, or does it make them feel like an outsider? Empowered, or weakened? Does it give them a sense of identity, or take their individualism away from them?

BEHAVIOUR EXPECTATIONS AND CODES OF CONDUCT

Even if your institution doesn't have a formal set of rules laid out, there are likely to be certain behaviour expectations. A mother shushing a child during a ritual or service. A follower giving a polite bow to a leader to show respect. Magic practitioners not using their powers to steal or cheat.

Of course, when there are rules and expectations, there are also consequences when people go against them. From nudging, staring, and shaking heads, up to expulsion, torture, or even death. How are those caught stepping out of line, brought back into it? How swiftly? How severely? How publicly?

I'm not going to go too deeply into the punishments side of things now, because we have a whole section on that coming up. So let's get back to what people should and shouldn't be doing.

Alongside a formal, written code, there may be additional expectations that haven't been formalised. While the formal rules may have specific consequences, whether carried out by people, spirits, deities, the informal expectations might be policed and punished in a more casual way.

There may be inequality in these expectations; with certain people held to a higher standard than others. Perhaps leaders are expected to set an example, and receive harsher punishments for indiscretions. Perhaps younger people are given more chances than their elders. Maybe more is expected of women, or of men, or of mothers, or those within particular high-profile families.

There may be rules that appear trivial, or don't have a clear purpose. There may be rules that are petty, and over the top. Maybe some are prejudice, or excluding. Some might be outdated, and no longer fit into the institution, or wider society. In which case, they may have been dropped from the official list of rules. Or the list may have been condensed over time to a shorter list, or just a singular, overarching rule, encouraging kindness, thoughtfulness, and love. Or, in fact, the opposite.

Consider who created these rules. Perhaps they were laid out by the founder, or by deities, or perhaps the source of them has been long-forgotten. Maybe each newly appointed leader is offered the chance to add or change a rule, or to rewrite them completely.

Perhaps the rules stand as a barrier between your protagonist and their goal. Perhaps it is the breaking of these rules that sets them out on their journey. Maybe they fight against them, campaigning for change. Perhaps they are forced to carry out a punishment, and that changes things for them.

Always keep in mind the aims and objectives of the institution, and how the rules uphold that. How they enforce it, and perpetuate it.

GENDER ROLES

Think about the different roles people have in your institutions that depend on their gender. Remember, when we're talking about gender, you need to consider transgender and non-binary characters too.

You may have institutions that only allow one gender entry to them. You may have areas, or clubs or societies within them that only accept one gender. Perhaps only men can become leaders, perhaps only women can become healers.

As with the codes of conduct, there may be gender rules that are enshrined within the rules of the institution, and there may be unspoken rules that are simply adhered to. Most of the time, at least.

Your institutions may be going through a time of transition, with a fight for equality. Such changes might be a decision to divide an institution forever, to break it into pieces.

Perhaps people are segregated based on gender, with students schooled separately, or with people worshipping or practising magic separately.

There might be practical reasons for the segregation. Maybe particular magical abilities are only present in one gender. This is a time to consider your transgender and non-binary characters, and how they fit in, and how they cope with it. And what happens when there's an anomaly, and someone is born with traits they shouldn't have?

Other separation of roles might be based on the perceived traits of the different genders. On stereotypical ideas, or on old-fashioned values.

Are the gender roles within your instituction aligned with the rest of society? Have they fallen behind, or are they forging ahead, waiting for the wider world to catch up? Perhaps they go against the mould entirely, with, for example, a matriarchal institution within a patriarchal world.

Maybe, for an oppressed or minority gender, the institution is something of a sanctuary; somewhere they can relax, be themselves, and have a bigger role. Or perhaps the institution is where they have to hide, to pretend to be something they're not, or are left feeling frustrated and held back.

Have things changed over the years, offering more diversity and more freedom? Has everything stayed stubbornly the same, with the same expectations and restrictions perpetuated? How does it affect your protagonist, and are they willing to challenge it?

PREJUDICE AND INEQUALITY

Does your institution assist in causing and maintaining inequality? Does it promote prejudice and exclusion? Beyond gender division, your institution may have a hand, either openly, or more subtly, in discriminating against people because of race, religion, skin colour, age, socio-economic status, physical ability, sexuality.

It may have an interest in maintaining the status quo of inequality, or an interest in appeasing the people who have an interest in maintaining it. Who funds your organisation? Where are its investments and financial interests? And what does it do to keep them?

Prejudice and inequality can come from many different places in your institution. It may be purposeful, in order to keep those in power in power. Or it may be more accidental. A misinterpretation of sacred texts, or the unnecessary clinging to rules written for people living centuries ago, when the world was a very different place. It may be prejudice that has travelled down through the generations without anyone really noticing it, or without enough people challenging it. It might be hidden behind a protection of the 'traditions' and 'history' of the institution.

When no one stands against inequality and prejudice, or the voices against aren't loud enough, then it stagnates and perpetuates. Generally, people don't like to examine their own prejudice and privelege. It's uncomfortable and confronting, and forces people to admit shameful things about themselves; their thoughts and actions. It causes guilt, and takes effort to change and re-write a deeply ingrained narrative. It's far easier to ignore it, pretend it's not there, and say nothing. To dress it up as 'not my fight', or 'not my story to tell'.

Of course, your institutions might wear their prejudice proudly, shouting it out, demonstrating against equality. It may be one of their core principles, and they may be very committed to keeping certain people out, or down. Or to eradicating them altogether.

Alternatively, an institution might purposefully keep away from equality battles. They might stay silent to hide a secret, shameful past of prejudice. They might try to distance themselves from atrocities and brutalities against minority groups by ignoring it. Staying away, and not tugging at that loose thread. Or they might stand at the forefront of a fight for equality in order to separate themselves from that past. To try and make up for it, to prove that they have changed (whether they have, or not.)

Also, within an institution, you are going to have different views. Everyone is an individual, with their own thoughts, and you're likely to have a full spectrum of people who want more equality, those who don't care, and those who are against it. It might cause an institution to break apart, separating into sub-groups with different agendas.

Perhaps your protagonist is only just seeing the prejudice in their institution, and in themselves. Perhaps they are being discriminated against, or they are determined to be an ally to those who are. Are they ready to stand against everything they've been told to believe in? Everything they're meant to be?

EDUCATION AND INSTRUCTION

Education and instruction happens in a number of different ways, and in a number of different settings. It might be parents teaching children at home, it might be a formal, official educational institution, it may be classes held at a religious or magic building, or it might be someone researching for themselves, using books or the internet.

When you're thinking about education and instruction, consider all the different types that might exist in a student's life. They might be taught magic or particular beliefs in school, go home to instruction from parents, attend weekend lessons at a religious or magical institution, and spend their own time researching. All of these different inputs might complement one another, teaching a single belief structure. However, they might contradict and oppose one another, leaving the student to struggle to find meaning and truth by themselves.

Education isn't always in the best interests of the student. It might be propaganda, or based in ignorance. It might be misleading, prejudice, one-sided, or it might be straight-up lying.

The formal education system in your world might be based on the government's narrative; specifically designed to create compliant, hard-working labourers who don't question anything. Or it might be designed to create soldiers, full of hate and propaganda. It might conflict with what people are learning in other institutions, or from their parents. What kind of inner turmoil might that create? And what happens to the one family member who believes a different narrative?

More internal conflict can be caused if students learn in school that the belief structure or magic system they're a part of is wrong, or evil, or lying to them. How do they decide who to believe? How do they find out the truth, without slant or prejudice?

Also consider who is able to receive education, and what level that education might be. In your world, girls might not have access to schools, putting the responsibility on their parents. Or only wealthy children might be able to go to school, or to continue attending school after the age of 12. Perhaps children within particular institutions are only allowed to receive an education via that institution, with access to other educational resources banned. Certain people may have access to a better, more comprehensive education than others.

Consider what knowledge may have been lost over the years. Consider what has been removed from and added to the curriculum. How have the changes in society or politics changed what students are taught, or how they are taught, or who is taught?

Is education a right in your world, or is it a privilege? Perhaps it isn't valued at all, with those seeking knowledge ridiculed and dissuaded from it. Maybe it is viewed as precious and valuable, with students willing to risk anything, even their lives, to receive it.

INITIATION

At some point, the followers of your institution may officially become members. Accepted, and initiated as a fully-participating affiliate.

This moment may come at their birth, or at some point within their first few months of life. It might be something they have no say in, and will never remember. It might be something that happens later in their childhood; as they enter their teens, or when they have their first period, or when their magical powers mature. This might be something they're given the responsibility to choose for themselves, or it might be a choice for their legal guardian.

Maybe the initiation comes at the beginning of adulthood, when they come of age. It might be after a graduation, or the appointment of their first official 'job' within the institution. They may be required to prove themselves in some way, to pass a test or challenge. Maybe it's a show of strength, or intelligence. Maybe they have to suffer a public humiliation, or receive a beating. Perhaps they have to commit a crime. Perhaps they have to kill.

Initiation ceremonies may be formal occasions, performed as a rite of passage in front of other members or leaders. It might be a moment for the family photo album. A time to dress up, to serve food, and bring people together.

Alternatively, it might be a secretive, or solo endeavour. Perhaps the initiate is sent away to complete their task, only proving themselves worthy if they return. Perhaps it the initiation happens in private, with everyone bound by secrecy, so that the ceremony remains mysterious and terrifying to those yet to experience it.

There may even be both kinds of initiation. An official one that the whole community attends, and a secondary one, carried out behind closed doors or at night. A brutal one, a degrading one, an illegal one. Carried out by bullies seeking to assert their power and control. It might be the leaders, or such initiations may be carried out without their knowledge. Or perhaps they simply choose to turn a blind eye. Put it down to 'hi-jinks' and 'harmless fun'. Until, that is, someone dies.

Maybe your protagonist is heading towards their initiation. How are they feeling about it? Do they feel ready? Do they know what's going to happen to them? Are they secure in the knowledge that they'll survive it?

COMING OF AGE

Members of your institutions may go through a coming of age ceremony, or, indeed, more than one.

It may be no more than a mention during a service, followed by slaps on the back, handshakes, maybe some small gifts of money. It may be a whole ritual, a celebration, or, as we've already discussed, an initiation task.

Coming of age ceremonies will happen at significant points in someone's youth, but it isn't necessarily going to be dictated by their physical age. Perhaps, within your magic system, members have one ceremony when their magical powers become evident, maybe during puberty, and have a second ceremony when they graduate from the magical academy, signifying their transition into adulthood.

When someone comes of age, they may be expected to take on certain roles and responsibilities. They may be expected to adhere to a new set of behaviour rules. They might be expected to find a partner, to move away from home, to devote themselves to their beliefs, or to lose their virginity.

Consider who goes through the coming of age ceremonies, and how they might differ for people. Perhaps girls and boys are treated differently. Perhaps rich and poor. Maybe those who have family members among the institution's leadership.

Why might one child dread coming of age, while another can't wait? What happens to children who don't meet the requirements to move to the next stage?

As ever, think about how these ceremonies and markers have changed over time. Have the ages been changed to adapt to children maturing faster? Maybe girls are partnered off younger in a world where the birth rate has fallen dramatically. Perhaps boys are sent to their professions later as technology advances and the labour market requires a higher level of training.

Consider which practices may have fallen out of favour as society changes. Maybe some have become illegal, despite still being practised in smaller, rural communities. Perhaps the law turns a blind eye, allowing outdated, discriminatory, or brutal practices to continue for the sake of 'tradition'. Or to keep the peace. Or to prevent from having to force their way into a closed institution. Or one that the government favours.

PUNISHMENT AND SANCTUARY

When people break the rules, there are consequences. And, for members of your institutions, there are two sets of rules they might break: those rules set by the institution themselves, and the law of the wider society they are also a part of. Those two sets of rules might complement one another, they might be quite similar. Or they may oppose one another.

By imposing rules upon your characters, you can increase the tension, and create conflict for them. By giving their actions consequences, and imposing punishments, you can raise the stakes. Remember: there are worse things that you can do to your character besides killing them.

Banishment, exclusion, the removal of magical powers can all be worse than death for your characters. Their punishment being borne by loved ones, or their shame falling, also, upon their family, can be worse. The removal of a treasured object, or the removal of access or other privileges.

What is the most precious thing in the world for your protagonist? Receiving a particular punishment may be a barrier to them achieving their overall goal. It might be something they have to overcome, or it could derail them entirely, leaving them to rethink their approach, to back-peddle, or to change their goal altogether. Or the punishment might be the inciting incident that sets them on their journey in the first place.

On the other hand, your characters might break a law of the land, and seek sanctuary within the institution. Will it hide them? Or will it hand them over? If the law broken stands in opposition to the institution's values, they may well find the sanctuary they're looking for. But, if the law matches the beliefs of your institution, civic duty and morality is likely to win.

Consider whether your institution would be happy to oppose the authority of the country; the police, the military, the government. Would they fight for their institution's privacy, blocking their requests to access, to search, to investigate? Does your institution have an interest in keeping the peace, in toeing the line?

Maybe the only sanctuary your protagonist can find is with the people they have always thought of as 'the other', or even 'the enemy'. Perhaps they are left with little choice but to seek hospitality from a rival institution, or accept the help that is offered to them.

Where can they be safe? Who can they trust?

AFTERLIFE: ETERNAL REWARDS AND DAMNATIONS

The eternal question: what happens after we die?

While the answer to this question can differ person to person, your institutions may have an official stance. Perhaps it teaches in the binary: one place for good people to go, another place for the sinners. Maybe the segregation isn't based on good and bad behaviour. Perhaps there's some kind of trial, allowing you to make good on your mistakes before moving on to some kind of eternity. Maybe the dead are held in stasis, until some future uprising event. Maybe they teach reincarnation, or transformation. Perhaps they believe that this one life is all you get.

If there is a belief in some kind of afterlife, what is the purpose of this life? Maybe it's some kind of trial, in which you need to prove yourself worthy. Maybe you earn 'points' with the choices you make, to cash in after death. Perhaps it's a test run, a suffering, a punishment to burn off some kind of original sin.

When you're thinking about the afterlife, consider how it attaches to your creation story. Consider how it promotes the ideals of your institutions, or satisfies their agendas.

Does the afterlife belief encourage hard work and devotion? Does it encourage putting up with hardships on promise of everlasting rewards? Perhaps it encourages kindness or love. Perhaps it encourages the pursuit for power and wealth.

It may be that, in your world, people have been there and come back. It may simply be near-death experiences, and stories that are easily dismissed. Or, perhaps, someone has returned from the afterlife with real, hard, and undeniable proof. How has that impacted institutions and society at large?

Perhaps members of your institutions converse with the dead. Maybe they practise mediumship, maybe they hold seances, maybe they can bring the dead back to life. Maybe the dead never actually leave, and walk alongside living people, either visible or not.

The curtain between the physical world and the spirit world may be incredibly thin, with spirits passing through with relative ease. Perhaps there is no contact, and no hope of getting a glimpse of it before coming back.

Think about how real the afterlife is. Is it nothing more than stories and superstitions, or is it a very real, sometimes visible, maybe even visitable, place? How does this change things for your characters? Could someone step into the afterlife to bring someone back? Do they have no fear of death?

How confident are they in their beliefs, or that they will be receiving eternal rewards, rather than an eternity of pain?

You've already laid out your institutions code of conduct for this lifetime, but what about the next? What are the deeds that will lead to damnation, and is there any hope of atonement? Consider the institution's agenda; its ultimate sins may be used to validate its prejudices and discriminations. Perhaps homosexuality will see a person damned, or suicide, or changing their body with tattoos, piercings, self harm, addiction, or gender reassignment. Maybe sex outside of marriage, abortion, second marriages.

Consider who is more likely to fall foul of these laws, and how unfair they might be. Perhaps a man who rapes a woman will still have a chance at redemption, but the woman who aborts a rapist's baby is beyond saving.

If your institution can point to a passage in a sacred text, stating that this act or that act will result in eternal suffering, they can justify discrimination as compassion, as an attempt to 'save' people.

Perhaps your institution stands firm on not judging people themselves. Perhaps someone's fate is only to be decided by some higher power. Is that higher power forgiving and merciful, or strict and ruthless?

Maybe there are acts that, no matter what has happened before, will guarantee them a place in some eternal paradise. Or guarantee them a return to earth. Maybe sacrificing their life for another's, maybe celibacy, maybe killing enemies of the true path.

What promises are made to believers? What threats are laid before them? Is it enough to keep people in line, or is the temptation too much?

A WORD ON INFO DUMPING AND LEARNING CURVES

Once you have completed your worldbuilding, and you are ready to start writing your book, you need to consider how, and how much, of this information to include.

Don't think that you will be including every ounce of what you've worked on. You won't. You shouldn't. I know, I know, you worked hard on it, but it wasn't wasted, even if it never makes it into your book. It helped you to understand your world, so that you can write about it in an informed, attached, and immersive way. So that you can make it all the more real for your readers.

An 'info dump' is the term used for when a writer pours out information onto the page as if they are writing a history text book. It's dry, it's dull, and, more often than not, it's confusing.

I'm sure you will have heard the old adage 'show don't tell'. This means that you should be *showing* your readers your worldbuilding, through action and dialogue, not simply *telling* them via a historical lecture.

The absolute best way to teach your readers about your world, is through action. This might be your character clashing with police, or it may simply be them navigating the world.

Let me expand on that: if something in your world is absolutely normal, however far removed it is from our world, if you character treats it, and reacts to it, as if it is entirely regular and everyday, then you are teaching your readers about your world through action.

Say, for example, centaurs are a common sight in your world. If your character treats them with no surprise at all, talking to them as if they are another human, then your readers learn that centaurs and humans live alongside one another equally. Or, perhaps your character ridicules, or bullies the centaurs. Or they treat them with respect, or fear. This is what you are teaching your readers about what is the norm in your world. Through action. This is the ideal way to show your worldbuilding.

It's not always so easy.

And so, the next best way is through dialogue. Again, avoid huge blocks of information. This is no different to info dumping, you're simply letting the history lecture come out of a character's mouth. However, they can have a conversation with a friend about a historical aspect of the world, or a cultural aspect. A conversation. Not a lecture.

Sometimes, however, you need to break the rules.

I'm not saying that you must never simply tell your readers information. Sometimes, it's necessary. Sometimes, it's even the better option. But, do it with careful consideration, and do it sparingly. Rules are, certainly in creative pursuits, meant to be broken.

If you're concerned about whether or not you're getting the balance right, the best way is through the use of beta readers. Beta readers read through early, pre-publication versions of books, and give honest feedback that allows the author to improve their story. If you've got the balance wrong, beta readers can tell you.

Another way to learn this is through reading, reading, and reading. Take careful note of how other authors handle the dilemma. How they get the balance right, and how they get it wrong.

The other way is simply through practice. The more you write, the more you drill down into your personal style and voice, the better you are likely to get at it.

The way in which you give worldbuilding information to your readers also depends on the complexity of your world, and how different it is to ours.

If you're writing about earth, whether in the present, past, or future, there are many things your readers will already know. They understand about time, and seasons. They know the animals, the plants. They know what humans are like, and how they interact. The learning curve of your world may be quite a gentle one.

Everything in your world that is different to our real world, adds to the learning curve of your book. Every mythical creature, every imagined technology, every drop of magic, and every jargon word makes that curve a little bit steeper.

You want to ease your readers in. If, in chapter one, you expect them to learn everything about your world and its history, learn who the characters are, and absorb their struggles and goals, they will be exhausted by the time they get to chapter two.

Tell them what they need to know. They don't need 5 million years worth of military history. They may need flashes of it, but not the entire thing. Be gentle with them. Don't make them do too much work, and don't leave them floundering around your story loaded down with too much knowledge.

Again, these are things that you can learn and improve on with the help of beta readers, by reading, reading, reading, and by simply practising your craft. You will find your way, I promise, but I can't tell you how to do it, because we are all different. And our stories are different. And our voices are different.

You might write short, 50,000 word novels, and leave a lot of the deeper worldbuilding out. You might write 130,000 word epics, with readers who expect a much more immersive experience. Practice, experiment, and you'll find the right balance for you, your books, and your readers.

IDEAS DUMP

As you work your way through this book, you are bound to have flashes of ideas popping into your mind. Character and story ideas, that don't quite belong with the workbook prompts.

Don't lose them; those little flashes are important.

Instead, use the following pages as something of an ideas dump. Some of these may never make it into your finished book, but, you never know, you may be able to recycle them into other stories.

No idea is ever wasted...

WANT EVEN MORE WORLDBUILDING?

Our adventures don't have to end here...

You can explore the rest of my series of worldbuilding guides for authors, guiding you through the basics of worldbuilding, helping you to create magic systems and religions, to write dystopian and post-apocalyptic fiction, and to create histories rich with myths and monsters.

Find more information on all of my workbooks and other worldbuilding services at angelinetrevena.co.uk/worldbuilding

Get Your Free Creating a Timeline Worksheet

Join my worldbuilding mailing list to claim your free Creating a Timeline worksheet.

You will also receive all the latest news on releases and workshops, as well as worldbuilding tips, tricks, and resources.

Join at subscribepage.com/worldbuilding

ABOUT ANGELINE TREVENA

Angeline Trevena was born and bred in a rural corner of Devon, but now lives among the breweries and canals of central England with her husband, their two sons, and a rather neurotic cat. She is a dystopian urban fantasy and post-apocalyptic author, a podcaster, and events manager.

In 2003 she graduated from Edge Hill University, Lancashire, with a BA Hons Degree in Drama and Writing. During this time she decided that her future lay in writing words rather than performing them.

Some years ago she worked at an antique auction house and religiously checked every wardrobe that came in to see if Narnia was in the back of it. She's still not given up looking for it.

Find out more at www.angelinetrevena.co.uk

Printed in Great Britain
by Amazon

11434622R00079